The Unexpected Rescue
of God's Children

Other books by Elizabeth Viera Talbot

Matthew: Prophecy Fulfilled

John: God Became Flesh

ELIZABETH VIERA TALBOT

Surprised by Love

Pacific Press® Publishing Association
Nampa, Idaho
Oshawa, Ontario, Canada
www.pacificpress.com

Cover design by Gerald Lee Monks
Cover design resources *Little One* © 2009 Jay Bryant Ward
Inside design by Aaron Troia
Outside editor: Aivars Ozolins

Additional copies of this book are available by calling toll-free 1-800-765-6955 or by visiting http://www.adventistbookcenter.com.

The author assumes full responsibility for the accuracy of all facts and quotations as cited in this book.

Unless otherwise noted, all Scriptures quoted are from *The New American Standard Bible*®, copyright © 1960, 1962, 1963, 1968, 1971, 1972, 1973, 1975, 1977, 1995 by The Lockman Foundation. Used by permission.

Library of Congress Cataloging-in-Publication Data:

Talbot, Elizabeth Viera.
  Surprised by love : the unexpected rescue of God's children /
Elizabeth Viera Talbot.
     p. cm.
  ISBN-13: 978-0-8163-2424-8 (pbk.)
  ISBN-10: 0-8163-2424-7
  1. Economy of God. 2. Salvation—Seventh-day Adventists. 3.
Seventh-day Adventists—Doctrines. I. Title.
  BX6154.T35 2010
  234—dc22
                                                      2010022137

11 12 13 14 • 5 4 3 2

edication

I dedicate this booklet to those, who
in various pivotal times in my life, have *rescued* me
by sharing their wisdom, support, and love:

My Old Testament professor, Dr. John Hartley,
who explained to me the concept of Jesus
as Kinsman-Redeemer, which forever
changed my life and ministry.

My loving husband, Patrick, who *really*
understands Jesus as our Redeemer,
and shares my passion to proclaim Him.

My uncles and aunts who offered a
"rescuing" hand during difficult times,
Dr. and Mrs. Robert and Shirley Torrey,
Dr. and Mrs. Antonio and Vivian Robles.

My beloved grandmother, "Omama,"
Alicia de Meier, who always comforted
me with her loving and wise advice.

My ex-boss and close friend,
Raffi Saboundjian, who provided
unconditional help when I needed it most.
My dear friend, Dr. Aivars Ozolins,
who always rescues me by editing
my manuscripts, and does it with a smile.

My parents, Dr. and Mrs. Juan Carlos and Alicia Viera,
whose selfless love for me gifted me with the
enacted visualization of how much God really loves me.

And as always to Jesus,
my Kinsman-Redeemer,
my *Go'el,* the One and Only.
I can't wait to see You face-to-face!

$\mathcal{T}$able of Contents

Chapter 1

The Children

Do you remember the first time you held a baby in your arms? Remember the first time you held *your* baby? The countless nights you sat by the crib and watched your baby breathe? It's hard to put our feelings into words when we talk about our babies, our children. Even as they grow and go through the difficult teenage years, even when they don't behave the way we hoped they would, we still sneak into their bedrooms at night to caress their hair, because they won't let us caress them when they are awake. They are the apples of our eyes, our greatest treasures, and our ultimate pleasure. Our love for them would make us climb mountains, cross rivers, and

> What would you be willing to give up to rescue her? Your honor? Your wealth? Your life?

face all kinds of perils. We think about our children when we are awake and dream about them at night (sometimes we dream about them during the day as well). They are everything to us. EVERYTHING!

How would you feel if one day your child was taken from you? What would you do if a kidnapper came along and convinced your child to follow him, deceiving her by telling her that you no longer have her best interest in mind and that you are keeping her from true happiness? What would you be willing to give up to rescue her? Your honor? Your wealth? Your life? All of the above?

This booklet is the story of God and His children: His love for them, His excitement to have them, and His plan to be together with them all through eternity. And it is also a story about the kidnapping of God's children and what He did and what He gave up in order to rescue them. He simply refused to go through eternity without them—without you and without me. He gave up EVERYTHING so that He could be reunited with us!

Preparing their home

"In the beginning God created the heavens and the earth" (Genesis 1:1). These seven Hebrew words that

> *G*od was preparing a *perfect* place for His children; they were the crown of His creation.

make up the first sentence in the Scriptures foreshadow the seven days of the creation process. God was preparing a *perfect* place for His children; they were the crown of His creation. As God was speaking their home into existence, He was also making qualitative statements about how well things were going. After the second day, "It was good" is found at the completion of every day, signifying that God was pleased with how earth was becoming the ideal home for *His babies.* Each day starts with "then God said," and it ends with "there was evening and there was morning." Every day God gave a command, and the narrative highlights the accomplishment of each command as we get closer and closer to *the day* when His children would arrive.

By the end of the fifth day, there was light; the expanse that separated the waters; dry land and seas; all

Can you feel God's excitement as He prepared for the next day? Do you remember when you prepared your home for your baby?

kinds of vegetation, plants, and fruit trees; luminaries in the firmament; living creatures in the waters; and birds in the air (see Genesis 1:1–23). How would you like *that* for a home? Can you feel God's excitement as He prepared for the next day? Do you remember when you prepared your home for your baby? How your heart was beating faster, how you could hardly wait?

The day has arrived!

The narrative clearly and repeatedly highlights the importance of the sixth day over the previous five days of Creation. For example, in the Hebrew, this is the first time the definite article *the* is used with a Creation day: a first day, a second day, a third day, a fourth day, a fifth day, *the* sixth day (see Genesis 1:31). *The day* has arrived!

On the sixth day, the goal of Creation would be revealed and the crowning piece manifested. Of all the days of Creation week, the sixth receives the longest coverage in the narrative. There is a two-part creation in this day; in the first part, God made the living creatures, the beasts of the earth, and, once again He assesses His work and says that "it was good" (Genesis 1:24, 25).

And then . . .

It was time! God was about to create His children— His babies. From this moment on, everything would be different. His universe would change forever. Their home was ready, the day had arrived. And God paused.

A divine counsel took place *exclusively* before creating humankind in the Creation narrative. As God is dialoguing in community, we get a glimpse of the uniqueness

> *God* was about to create His children—
>
> His babies. From this moment on,
>
> everything would be different.

and climactic significance of this moment: "Then God said, 'Let Us make man' " (Genesis 1:26). "Man" (*'adam*) is a collective name for humankind, as will be further explained in Genesis 1:27. God has reflected and decided to have children. You can almost picture in your mind a husband and wife in intimate conversation at the kitchen table, planning the most important decision of their lives: "Let's have children."

God's children would be in *His* image: "Let Us make man in Our image, according to Our likeness; and let them rule over the fish of the sea and over the birds of the sky and over the cattle and over all the earth, and over every creeping thing that creeps on the earth" (Genesis 1:26). Humankind would bear God's image and likeness; humans would be like God but not identical to God; in His image and likeness, but not gods. God had made the decision. In Genesis 1:26, we hear the voice of God in the first person. Then the narrator poetically re-

> *He* created a male and a female *'adam*.

ports the creation of God's children in the third person, emphasizing that we were created in His image: "God created man in His own image, in the image of God He created him; male and female He created them" (Genesis 1:27). God is the only One who can "create" (*bara'*), this Hebrew verb is only used with God as a subject, no one else can "create." God's children are designated by gender, not by kinds or species like the animals. He created a male and a female *'adam*. The Creator created "procreators." Each gender was bestowed with amazing and unique characteristics for a complementary and complete view of the image of God. Amazing! You and I are in the image of God!

God's children are then invested with authority. Their two assignments are to multiply and to subdue the earth, ruling over the animals. Their diet is specified and animal meat consumption is not part of it (permission to eat meat

*Y*ou have children in your image. Humankind is created in the image of the Sovereign Creator.

will come from God after the Flood). They have access to every seed-bearing plant and every tree that has fruit. They have dominion over the rest of creation on earth; this is their home. They, and only they in all of creation, are in God's image. The concept of the *image of God* appears only four times in the Jewish Scriptures, and all four instances are found in Genesis (1:26, 27 [twice]; 9:6). They all relate to the creation of humankind. Later on, Adam would have a child "in his own likeness, according to his image" (Genesis 5:3). You have children in your image. Humankind is created in the image of the Sovereign Creator, and as such, God delegates His sovereignty and now His children are to rule the

*H*aving a garden is *good,* having a pet is *good.*

But having children is *very good*!

earth. They hold the highest place in the created order. Are you feeling pretty special by now?

Well, God thinks that His children are more than special. When He evaluates His creative work of the sixth

The Children

day, He can't just call it "good" as in all the other days. No! The plants and the animals are good, the children are VERY GOOD! "God saw all that He had made, and behold, it was *very good*. And there was evening and there was morning, *the* sixth day" (Genesis 1:31; emphasis added). Yes, having a garden is *good,* having a pet is *good*. But having children is *very good*! This was *the* day they came to life, and God would always remember it, the way you remember *the* day your children were born. That was the most important day in your life! And it was *very good*!

The nursery

The specifics of how God created humankind are further explained in Genesis 2. "Then the LORD God formed man of dust from the ground, and breathed into

> *I* wonder if God kept looking at His child
> for a while before He breathed the breath
> of life into his nostrils.

his nostrils the breath of life; and man became a living being" (Genesis 2:7). God formed man (*'adam)* from the dust of the ground (*adamah*); notice the word relationship between the man and the ground. I wonder if God kept looking at His child for a while before He breathed the breath of life into his nostrils. I wonder if He observed the newly formed body on the ground as a parent observes his newly born baby. I wonder how God felt as

He envisioned an eternity together with His children, created in His image.

God also decided that it was not good for the male human to be alone. He also created a complementary, suitable companion for him: the female human. Together they would portray the image of God (see Genesis 1:27).

Do you remember how you prepared your child's nursery?

God fashioned the woman out of the man and brought her to him. He was ecstatic! He identified her as "bone of my bones, and flesh of my flesh" (Genesis 2:23). He called her "woman" (*ishah*) because he was "man" (*ish*) (verse 23); he wanted to identify her with him. He was *really* excited! I wish all husbands would show such excitement for their wives! They were naked together and they felt no shame (see Genesis 2:25). Talk about a perfect marriage relationship!

As a proud parent, God decided to make a special place for His children. The earth was now beautiful, filled with flowers, trees, animals, and so forth. But still, God wanted to create a very special space just for them, a place of pleasure for His children, a nursery. Do you remember how you prepared your child's nursery? Remember how you chose the perfect color for her bedroom? How you stood in the middle of the room, considering the appropriate place for the rocking chair, the diaper table, the tiny gym; how you were deciding where to place all the stuffed animals and what to hang from the ceiling for your baby's delight. Well, so did God.

"The LORD God planted a garden toward the east, in Eden; and there He placed the man whom He had formed. Out of the ground the LORD God caused to grow every tree that is pleasing to the sight and good for food" (Genesis 2:8, 9). Oh, this was such a special nursery! God planted the beautiful Garden just for His babies' delight. He *placed* humans in this unique place that He had de-

> The Garden of Eden was, in the fullest sense of the expression, the "Paradise of delight." Of course! What else would God give His children?

signed for them. Can you imagine God planting trees that were not just good for food, but *pleasing* to the sight so that His children would delight in the beauty that surrounded them? Just like you did for *your* children, who are in *your* image.

This nursery garden was the place of ultimate beauty. In the ancient Semitic language of the Mediterranean Sea, the root word for *Eden* means "delight." Furthermore, when the Jewish Scriptures (Old Testament) were translated into Greek, many years before Jesus Christ was born, the Greek word for "garden" utilized in Genesis 2:8, 9 was *paradeisos*. The Garden of Eden was, in the fullest sense of the expression, the "Paradise of delight." Of course! What else would God give His children?

In the midst of the *paradeisos,* God placed the "tree of life" (Genesis 2:9). The fruit of the tree of life was a visual and tactile reminder of the children's connection with the Life-Giver. They were created to be eternal, just as God is eternal. They would eat and live forever. That's who they were and that was the plan! We have eternity placed deep in the core of our souls, because we were made in the image of the Everlasting God.

First things first

Now that His children had come to life, the creation process was complete; it was done, finished, and perfect. It was time to celebrate! God ceased His work and blessed and sanctified the seventh day; the day that forever would point to the completeness and wholeness of God's creation. The seventh day would be perpetually linked with Creation and Redemption. But wait! We haven't discussed Redemption yet. It's coming up in the next few chapters—and I can't wait to tell you about it!

Humans were the children of God. And as such, they spent the very first day of their lives together with the Creator in the special Garden made for them, celebrating the completeness of God's creation, of which they were the crowning masterpiece. The seventh day was *the* first day the Creator and His children spent together in intimate communion. "By the seventh day God completed

His work which He had done, and He rested on the seventh day from all His work which He had done. Then

> *G*od did not just want a birthday celebration once a year—He wanted us to remember *every week, on the seventh day.*

God blessed the seventh day and sanctified it, because in it He rested from all His work which God had created and made" (Genesis 2:2, 3). The Creator and His creatures rested together. Wouldn't you have done the same? Don't you love to take time to celebrate together with your children? Well, God did not just want a birthday celebration once a year—He wanted us to remember *every week, on the seventh day.* So, He set it apart and made it holy. His children would have a constant reminder that He was their Creator.

Your worth in God's eyes

In the ancient cultures of Egypt and Mesopotamia, the designation of being "in the image of God" was reserved exclusively for prominent people: kings, important officers, and royal rulers. The Genesis narrative emphasizes that God did not make such distinctions. When God decided to create mankind in His own image, He did not make some people more special than the others— He did not separate them by hierarchy and power. *Every human being* bears the image of God. The royal language is used for every child of God, regardless of status, caste, gender, or position in society. YOU are a child of God! We are His royal children!

What are your children worth to you? Well, then maybe you are starting to get a glimpse of God's love for you and me. God rejoices over us with singing and shouts of joy (see Zephaniah 3:17), just like you sing for joy when you think of your children. And even so, God loves His children even more than we do.

> "Can a woman forget her nursing child
> And have no compassion on the son of her womb?
> Even these may forget, but I will not forget you.
> "Behold, I have inscribed you on the palms of
> My hands" (Isaiah 49:15, 16).

Take a moment to thank your Creator. Thank Him for deciding to have children in His image. Thank Him for loving us with a love so great that we can't even fully comprehend it. Tell Him how much you love Him be-

Every human being bears the image of God.

cause He first loved you. And if you think that your efforts to communicate with Him are not good enough to reach the Almighty God, or that your failures make you unattractive to your Creator, just look at your refrigerator. Look at those simple drawings that your children made for you. The one that says, "Mommy, I LOVE YOU." Isn't that messy colored paper the most beautiful work of art you've ever seen?

Chapter 2

The Kidnapping

When I was a little girl, my father was a church administrator. He was the top denominational official for a geographical area consisting of three countries. The country where we were residing at the time was not my dad's country of origin. This country was going through a difficult time of political upheaval that permeated many areas of our daily lives. One day, my dad received a letter in his office stating that he did not deserve to be the church's president in that area because he was not born in the country where the offices where now located. The letter gave my dad a few hours to leave the country.

Illogical letters such as this one would have been easily disregarded, except that this note carried a heavy consequence if my dad did not do as commanded; "they" (it was an anonymous letter) would kidnap me. I am an only child and "they" threatened to take me away from my parents forever. I still remember the concern in my parents' faces. They trusted in the Lord and were engaged in His work; what should they do? Having prayed earnestly, they decided not to heed this anonymous threat. My parents notified my school with the strictest of instructions: NOBODY—no one—other than my parents could pick me up from school, no matter who they claimed to be. During that time, I could not walk to school by myself, even though we lived three blocks from it. I was told not to engage in conversation with any adult under any circumstances.

You know the end of the story because I am still here, writing this booklet. The threat never became a reality. But it was a scary time for my parents; it was even scarier for them than for me because I was too young to understand what was going on and the consequences of being kidnapped.

God's children, whom He loved, who were created in His image for eternal intimacy with Him, were kidnapped.

Have you ever lost a child to a kidnapper? I certainly hope not. How about losing sight of your child for two minutes in a park or a mall? I have witnessed desperate mothers stop passersby with utter desperation in their faces, asking if the passersby had seen their child who had been next to them a moment before. There is nothing, absolutely nothing in this life as painful as losing a child. This chapter tells the saddest story of the world's history, when a kidnapper came along and convinced God's children to follow him. On that fateful day, God's children, whom He loved, who were created in His image for eternal intimacy with Him, were kidnapped. And the universe would never be the same.

To live or to die: That is the choice
When God created the "Paradise of delight" for His

children, He caused trees to grow for beauty and food. Two trees are highlighted in the Genesis narrative: "Out of the ground the Lord God caused to grow every tree that is pleasing to the sight and good for food; the tree of life also in the midst of the garden, and the tree of the knowledge of good and evil" (Genesis 2:9). In the Hebrew, it is emphasized that the tree in the middle of the Garden is the tree of life; it is placed in the center of Paradise. The other tree is close by (even though some English translations indicate that the latter was in the middle). The tree of life signified life and the connection of humankind to the Life-Giver. Eating from it would result in eternal life (see Genesis 3:22) as an experiential symbol of the gift of life they were given by the Creator. They were created for eternal life because they were children of the Eternal God.

The other was the tree of the knowledge of good and evil. It signified the death that comes with the knowledge

If humans ever decided to eat from this tree, it would be something like saying to God, "Thank You for Your wisdom, but, from now on, we think we can handle our moral development ourselves. Thank You but, no, thank You."

of evil if we refuse the moral discernment of the Life-Giver. This tree represented the choice of being morally independent, no longer relying on God, the Creator, for discernment of good and evil. If humans ever decided to eat from this tree, it would be something like saying to God, "Thank You for Your wisdom, but, from now on, we think we can handle our moral development ourselves. Thank You but, no, thank You." This tree was the visualization of wanting to be like gods, deciding what is good and what is evil. This tree is only mentioned by name (the tree of the knowledge of good and evil) two times in the Bible (Genesis 2:9, 17). The scarce usage of the name of this tree is in contrast with the tree of life, which is referred to many times in Genesis and other parts of the Bible, including the last book of the Bible (see, for example, Revelation 22:2, 14, 19).

Just like my parents lovingly protected me from the kidnapper by instructing me not to engage in conversations with strangers or get into unknown cars, God gave His beloved children directions on how to stay away from harm. Because humans were created as moral beings,

They were perfect moral beings who only knew good, but they could choose to leave God's umbrella of ethical discernment.

God would protect their freedom with a boundary, a very clear boundary. They would know exactly when they were crossing the line to moral independence. God gave them an umbrella permission with a prohibition that was the exception: "The LORD God commanded the man, saying, 'From any tree of the garden you may eat freely; but from the tree of the knowledge of good and evil you shall not eat, for in the day that you eat from it you will surely die' " (Genesis 2:16, 17). "Any tree" included the tree of life. Their default would be endless life, eating from all the other trees and the tree of life. But, if they chose to be like gods, thinking that they could discern what was good and what was evil, they would separate themselves from the Life-Giver's care and would be under the sentence of death. They were perfect moral beings who only knew good, but they could choose to leave God's umbrella of ethical discernment. To live or to die—that was their choice.

One year before I was born, my parents helped a family in extreme need. The local church was going to build a modest, small home for a single mother of shady reputation who had many children. The children were living in the most precarious situation, and it was no longer a healthy environment for them. They were regularly by themselves at night; all eight of them sleeping in the same little bed. The mattress had given way under the weight of the children, and all of them were now sleeping in a hollow in the middle of the bed. The same bed. The children were temporarily distributed among the church families, and my parents brought home a four-year-old little girl. She had never seen a bathtub before, and when my mom gave her a bath, she became extremely angry with my mom for doing such a thing to her! My mom then dressed her in beautiful pajamas and tenderly took her to bed. A bed for herself. But the little girl started crying because she was by herself and cold and uncomfortable because none of her brothers and sisters were in the same bed with her. By then, this little four-year-old girl thought she knew better than my parents what was good and what was evil for her. In no uncertain terms, she announced to my parents what she had decided to do with all this "mistreatment": she would gather all her little clothes and leave the house! Can you imagine? My parents told me this story and my heart went out to this little girl. At the same time, it gave me a glimpse of how foolish God's children acted that fateful day when they decided that they knew better than their Creator and chose moral independence. They decided to leave God's tender loving care behind and follow the kidnapper.

The kidnapper

The kidnapper and deceiver took upon himself the form of a serpent (see Genesis 3:1). This was an attractive sight because this animal was beautiful, and the first woman was mesmerized by it. She established a conversation with this beautiful animal without realizing that she was getting too close to trespassing the protective boundary.

Aside from the attractive beauty used by the deceiver, the kidnapper's tactics reflect well thought out, crafty methods. The first sentence spoken by the serpent is an expression of shock! And it comes with an *exaggeration* of God's words: "Indeed, has God said, 'You [all of you, second person plural] shall not eat from any tree of the garden'?" (Genesis 3:1). In our language, this expression would sound something like, "WOW! Did God REALLY

say that you couldn't eat from any tree in the Garden?"
Of course God had said exactly the opposite: they could
eat of any tree in the Garden except for one (see Genesis
2:16, 17). Kidnappers have always been, and always will
be, crafty deceivers.

Even though the kidnapper is having this conversation with Eve, the first woman (see Genesis 3:20), all the

In our language, this expression would sound
something like, "WOW! Did God REALLY say that
you couldn't eat from any tree in the Garden?"

pronouns—*you* and *we*—are plural because she is being
addressed as the representative of the first couple, and she
is answering for herself, for her husband, and, ultimately,
for humankind. She decides that she needs to "correct"
the kidnapper, because his statement is not true (which
should have been a hint of what was coming). The *correc-
tion* states, "From the fruit of the trees of the garden we
may eat; but from the fruit of the tree which is in the
middle of the garden, God has said, 'You shall not eat
from it or touch it, or you will die' " (Genesis 3:2, 3). The
first thing we notice is that she had been focusing on the
forbidden tree because she thinks that this tree is in the
middle of the Garden, when, in fact, the tree of life held
that central spot. Plus, she herself starts distorting and
exaggerating what God had commanded, because she
adds that God said not to "touch" the tree, a command

that was never recorded in the previous narrative. The tactics of the kidnapper are working, and she is starting to use his methods without recognizing the trap. God's little girl is in danger!

The kidnapper then makes a false *assertion,* just the opposite of what God had said. "The serpent said to the woman, 'You surely will not die!' " (verse 4). This is the greatest lie! God had said, "You will surely die" (Genesis 2:17). The deceiver then continues by explaining God's own thoughts, as if he was "unmasking" God's real motives: "For God knows that in the day you eat from it your eyes will be opened, and you will be like God, knowing

> The tactics of the kidnapper are working, and she is starting to use his methods without recognizing the trap. God's little girl is in danger!

good and evil" (Genesis 3:5). That was it! YOU can be gods, deciding for yourselves what is good and what is evil. You don't need the Creator anymore! You can have moral independence; you have discernment. Why are you putting up with all this mistreatment that is keeping you from your potential? Just pick up your clothes and leave this home! You can do better than this!

Sound familiar?

The woman took another look at the tree: "When the woman saw that the tree was good for food, and that it was a delight to the eyes, and that the tree was desirable

The Kidnapping

to make one wise" (Genesis 3:6). Make one wise? Where did she get THAT from? The first two assertions about the tree were true; those were the reasons why all the

> *Having* talked to the kidnapper, Eve was tricked into believing that she could have moral discernment without God, and would become "wiser."

trees were there: "Out of the ground the LORD God caused to grow every tree that is pleasing to the sight and good for food" (Genesis 2:9). But where did she pick up the *misperception* that aside from food and beauty this particular tree would make her wise? Well, from the kidnapper, of course. Now God's little girl was thinking like the deceiver. And she reached out and . . .

"She took from its fruit and ate; and she gave also to her husband with her, and he ate" (Genesis 3:6). NO! Why did they think *that* was wisdom? Why didn't they stay with the Source of wisdom and life? The description of Eve's and Adam's sin is narrated in eight words in the Hebrew language. Just eight words that would change the history of the universe. Having talked to the kidnapper, Eve was tricked into believing that she could have moral discernment without God, and would become "wiser." So she ate the forbidden fruit, breaching the boundary of God's protection, and she went to her husband and he also ate. Hers was the sin of initiative; his was the sin of compliance, a tacit consent.

God's children had been KIDNAPPED!

Consequences

"Then the eyes of both of them were opened, and they knew that they were naked; and they sewed fig leaves together and made themselves loin coverings" (Genesis 3:7). Both of them realized immediately that something had gone terribly wrong. They had been deceived! And now they realized that they were naked and, feeling shame, they covered themselves. The previous chapter had ended with NO shame: "And the man and his wife

> *They* wanted to know evil—now they did. From then on, fear, shame, and pain would be their constant companions. Theirs was a very, very sad story.

were both naked and were not ashamed" (Genesis 2:25). Now they saw themselves in a different light, and they felt the need to cover themselves and they thought that fig leaves would do the job just fine. (I wonder if fig leaves looked the same then as they do now because it doesn't sound like a good idea to me!)

The immediate consequences of the kidnapping were *shame, fear, blame,* and *pain.* Unfortunately, all of us know the meaning of these words very well. They wanted to know evil—now they did. From then on, fear, shame, and pain would be their constant companions. Theirs was a very, very sad story. The progression from shame to fear and then to blame may be clearly seen in their dialogue with God:

> Then the Lord God called to the man, and said to him, "Where are you?" He said, "I heard the sound of You in the garden, and I was afraid because I was naked; so I hid myself." And He said, "Who told you that you were naked? Have you eaten from the tree of which I commanded you not to eat?" The man said, "The woman whom You gave to be with me, she gave me from the tree, and I ate." Then the Lord God said to the woman, "What is this you have done?" And the woman said, "The serpent deceived me, and I ate" (Genesis 3:9–13).

It almost sounds like you are having a discussion with your children, doesn't it? You walk into the room and there is a big mess: paint on the walls, paint on their clothes, on their faces, EVERYWHERE! They are afraid

God does not curse His children.

He curses the serpent.

because they know they have done something wrong and they fear the consequences; they have shame so they are staring at the floor. When you ask questions, they start blaming each other. Our behavior hasn't changed much since that first time in Paradise, has it?

God does not curse His children. He curses the serpent (see Genesis 3:14). From now on, the serpent would no more be a beautiful animal. It would crawl on its belly and would eat dust (a symbol of humiliation). Then God informs the woman and the man that they would experience pain. Not only are they under a death sentence and have become mortals, but they would also experience pain while doing their originally assigned occupations: they would still multiply and fill the earth and they would still work the ground and eat from it, but they would have pain while doing it.

The woman would experience pain while giving birth, and sin would change the dynamic between husband and wife (see Genesis 3:16). There would be desire versus rule; the reciprocal marriage relationship that God had originally designed was now modified. The man would experience pain because the ground was now cursed and with pain (some versions translate this word as "toil," but it is the same word as the pain the woman would suffer) he would eat from it. With sweat in his face, it would be a hard working life (see Genesis 3:17–19). Furthermore, instead of being eternal, humans would return to dust at the end of their lives: "For you are dust, and to dust you shall return" (Genesis 3:19). It was a sad, sad day for the whole universe; the saddest day for God and His created children.

God's children had been deceived. They thought they could have the knowledge of good and evil. Now that they had claimed their "ethical independence" they were no longer under God's moral umbrella and thus not safe.

The Kidnapping

Therefore, they would not be allowed to continue eating from the tree of life (see Genesis 3:22–24). Now they had to leave the beautiful nursery God had prepared for them; the "Paradise of delight" would not be their special home

It was a sad, sad day for the whole universe; the saddest day for God and His created children.

anymore. I think this is the saddest summary in all of Scripture: "Therefore the LORD God sent him out from the garden of Eden, to cultivate the ground from which he was taken. So He drove the man out; and at the east of the garden of Eden He stationed the cherubim and the flaming sword which turned every direction to guard the way to the tree of life" (Genesis 3:23, 24). By their own choice, this was no longer their home. They would not be eating of the tree of life again. EVER! They were helpless and hopeless.

The unexpected promise

What would you do if your child ended up exactly where you told her not to go? What if your son talked to the kidnapper even though he wasn't supposed to? What would you do if your children were kidnapped? Would you say, "I told you so, now you are on your own"? I have a feeling that you would look desperately for a way to rescue your children. As a matter of fact, I know that you would live the rest of your days planning how to get your children back. Rescuing your children would become your passion and your obsession. And that is exactly what happened to God.

God spoke to the kidnapper with one of the most passionate prophetic statements in the Scriptures: "I AM going to CRUSH YOUR HEAD! You think you are getting away with this, think again! NO WAY! This is not the end! I am coming back for them! I simply refuse to spend eternity without my children!" The Hebrew Scriptures record this promise:

> "And I will put enmity
> Between you and the woman,
> And between your seed and her seed;
> He shall bruise you on the head,
> And you shall bruise him on the heel" (Genesis 3:15).

The serpent and its offspring would eventually bring much pain to the offspring of the woman. There would

This is not the end! I am coming back for them! I simply refuse to spend eternity without my children!"

be an ongoing conflict between the two. The seed of the serpent would crush the heel of the seed of the woman. BUT! The offspring of the woman would CRUSH THE SERPENT'S HEAD!

That was the plan. And from here onward, the rest of

• 36 •

the Bible is the story about exactly that—the rescue of God's children. It tells us about how and when it happened and gives us the assurance that the rescue is not only on the way, but that He has already accomplished it. I can't wait to tell you about it! I am SO excited! The plan would become known as "the covenant." God loved His children SO MUCH that He surprised them all.

Take a moment with God. Write a prayer of thanks-

> *That* was the plan. And from here onward, the rest of the Bible is the story about exactly that—the rescue of God's children.

giving to Him on a piece of paper. Try to imagine how desperate you would feel if you lost your children, and then thank Him for being even more desperate than you could ever possibly be. Then imagine what you would give up to get your babies back, and thank Him for giving up much more than you ever could. Then thank Him for that first promise that became our ONLY HOPE.

We were kidnapped, but He surprised us with His indescribable love. He would give up heaven to rescue us!

How does it feel to be loved THAT MUCH?

Chapter 3

The Rescuer

It was a sunny afternoon and my mother and I were really enjoying ourselves. We were in La Pampa, Argentina, a little town where my parents were conducting an evangelistic series. My dad was an evangelist and the three of us used to move to a new location every six months. Having arrived in a new town, my parents and the evangelistic team would spend the first two months settling in, getting to know the location and the people, advertising the upcoming meetings, and getting ready for them. The third and fourth months were devoted to the actual meetings, which usually took place every night in a big tent. During the last two months, a new church would be established, a meeting place secured, and a new minister assigned. Then we would move to the next location and start all over again. On that sunny afternoon, I was four years old and my mother had decided to take me for a ride.

We lived in a very small mud house. There was not much for me to do at home, so my mother borrowed a bicycle to take me for a fun sightseeing ride. I was so excited! I was not old enough to ride this bike myself, so I settled in a small seat behind my mother. She was the one in charge, pedaling and steering on our tour. I was the one enjoying it in the back. So we began. We had been going for quite a while and were now far away from the town, enjoying the never-ending wheat fields. At one point, on a particularly bumpy part of the road, I started to slide sideways off of the bike seat. My mother advised me to straighten up and to hold on firmly, so I wouldn't fall. And I did. And then it happened.

I started crying with utter desperation and my mom couldn't understand why. She stopped the bike and asked me why I was crying. I was unable to talk, but she saw that I was in severe pain. What was happening? She couldn't see anything wrong, but I kept pointing to my feet. I had socks that covered my legs almost up to my knees and my mom decided she had to take my socks off to find out what was going on. So she did. And then she saw it! The flesh at the bottom of my foot came off along with the sock, and she could see a white bone where my heel and my foot used to be.

As I had tried to straighten up on the seat, I had accidentally stuck my foot in the moving wheel, which had completely destroyed my foot. We were miles away from the little town we lived in, and even if we were there, they did not have an adequate medical facility to deal with something of

Have you ever needed a rescuer?

Someone who could do for you what

you could not do for yourself?

this magnitude. Plus, I couldn't move and was bleeding so heavily that my mom was afraid that I could bleed to death in no time, right there in the middle of nowhere.

The Rescuer

Have you ever needed a rescuer? Someone who could do for you what you could not do for yourself? Have you ever had your children in a similar situation, with YOU being the rescuer? Well, my mother didn't have to think about it twice. With energy and strength that seemed to come directly from above, my mom sat me on the main seat of the bicycle and took hold of the handlebars and started to run to take me back to town. I don't know how she ran all those miles or how she kept herself together. All she knew is that she needed to do for me what I couldn't do for myself. Save me. After all, I was her little girl!

Right outside the town, she saw an ill-equipped clinic that was designed to deal with simple ailments and minor injuries, the only medical facility the town had. We went inside and she asked for an X-ray. They explained to her that they were out of X-ray film but that she could leave me there and go to the other side of town to fetch the film from a pharmacy. She couldn't phone my dad because cellular phones didn't exist then (yes, I am that old). So she jumped on her bike, pedaling with all her strength in order to save her girl. I still remember sitting and waiting on that cold black table where they would take my X-ray once she would return with the film.

Finally, my mom came back and it turned out that I had no broken bones. It took me six months, though, to recover and get my foot back. There is a tiny little scar on my heel that reminds me of that fateful day—the day when my mom also became my rescuer, because she did for me what I couldn't do for myself. She ran for me because I had become handicapped; my feet could not run or pedal, so she used her feet to carry me. My mother had given me life in the first place when I was born, and now she had given me life all over again because she had rescued me from certain death.

Have you ever become your child's rescuer? In this chapter, I want to tell you of the incredible and unexpected way in which God became the Rescuer of His kidnapped children.

Closest of Kin

One of the most intriguing themes running through Scripture is the one commonly referred to as "Kinsman-Redeemer." When someone was in distress and in need of being rescued, his or her closest relative could legally step in. If a man could no longer support himself, he could give up his property or inheritance; and if that wasn't enough, he could sell himself as a slave to pay his debt. What a terrible situation! But wait! There was a light at the end of the tunnel! The nearest kinsman or closest relative could act on the victim's behalf; he could purchase the property or land and restore it to its original owner or pay the ransom for the enslaved relative to be set free. The *closest of kin* claimed responsibility for the relative in distress. Can you imagine being so destitute and so lost, and then you hear the news about your kinsman-redeemer on his way to rescue you? WOO-HOO! That's the only response I can think of.

The word in Hebrew for "kinsman-redeemer" is *Go'el.*

The Rescuer

The *Go'el* had many roles regarding the destitute relative. Leviticus 25 is one of the chapters to explain in detail some of the laws of redemption. I will highlight four of

> *O*ne of the most intriguing themes running
> through Scripture is the one commonly
> referred to as "Kinsman-Redeemer."

the *Go'el* roles, which inform our study, with a special emphasis on the first two.

1. To redeem property that was given up by a poor relative. "If a fellow countryman of yours becomes so poor he has to sell part of his property, then his nearest kinsman [*Go'el*] is to come and buy back what his relative has sold" (Leviticus 25:25). For further information, please see Leviticus 25:25–34.

2. To redeem a relative who had sold himself into slavery. "Now if . . . a countryman of yours becomes so poor with regard to him as to sell himself to a stranger who is sojourning with you, or to the descendants of a stranger's family, then he shall have redemption right after he has been sold. One of his brothers may redeem him, . . . or one of his blood relatives from his family may redeem him" (Leviticus 25:47–49). For further study, see Leviticus 25:47–54.

3. To avenge the blood of a murdered relative. The *Go'el haddam* was the "avenger of blood." The murderer, then, would only be safe in any of the cities of refuge (see Numbers

35:12, 19–27; Deuteronomy 19:6, 12; Joshua 20:2).

4. To appear in a lawsuit as a helper for a relative. The *Go'el* would make sure that justice was done (see Proverbs 23:11; Jeremiah 50:34; Psalm 119:154).

Can you imagine a person in slavery, destitute, without property, or in a lawsuit? Can you imagine the helplessness and the hopelessness the person experienced? But can you visualize the happiness and relief the same person started to feel when he or she saw the *Go'el*?

As a child I was in situations where I got desperate and felt hopeless and needed to find one of my parents. A particular situation stands out in my mind when I was sitting alone in a parked car and felt I was in grave danger (I wasn't, but I thought I was). Somehow, I managed to squeeze out through a half-opened window and wandered

Can you imagine a person in slavery, destitute, without property, or in a lawsuit? Can you imagine the helplessness and the hopelessness the person experienced? But can you visualize the happiness and relief the same person started to feel when he or she saw the Go'el?

around for about a block, crying and looking for my mom, until someone heard me and called her from a business appointment. As soon as I saw her, I felt safe. I still had tears in my eyes, but I felt safe (just like the image of the girl on this book's cover). I am sure that you have experienced it; the feeling you get when your children run to you and touch you to make sure you are next to them. Sometimes it happens when someone they don't know just smiles at them. They want to make sure you are next to them, then they can be brave enough to smile back.

The *Go'el* was the redeemer, the person who looked after your safety and did whatever was necessary to take your shame away and bring you back to freedom. Your closest of kin was your hope and safety.

If a person had no *Go'el* and lost everything, he or she still had ONE HOPE. Yahweh, the Lord, would be his or her ultimate *Go'el,* who would step in during the year of jubilee. Every seven times seven years, God would step in for everyone:

> " 'You are also to count off seven sabbaths of years for yourself, seven times seven years, so that you have the time of the seven sabbaths of years, namely, forty-nine years. You shall then sound a ram's horn abroad on the tenth day of the seventh month; on the day of atonement you shall sound a horn all through your land. You shall thus consecrate the fiftieth year and proclaim a release [or liberty] through the land to all its inhabitants. It shall be a jubilee for you, and each of you shall return to his own property, and each of you shall return to his family' " (Leviticus 25:8–10).

In the year of jubilee, then Yahweh Himself, by His

own legal right, would step in and become the Kinsman-Redeemer. Everyone became free. The concepts of the Sabbath day, the Sabbath year, the Day of Atonement,

> *T*he Go'el was the redeemer, the person who looked after your safety and did whatever was necessary to take your shame away and bring you back to freedom. Your closest of kin was your hope and safety.

and the year of jubilee would be forever linked to redemption. The captives were set free by Yahweh.

It is very interesting to me that the Liberty Bell, the symbol of freedom in the United States of America, has this very verse inscribed on it: *Lev. XXV:X Proclaim LIBERTY throughout all the land unto all the inhabitants thereof.* That is where the bell gets its name from.

Our *Go'el*

And this is where it gets really good! The next sentence is the most important one to understand in this whole booklet. So, read it twice if necessary.

When God created us in *His image,* He pledged Himself to a *rescue plan* because He was our *"closest of Kin."* He is our *Go'el.* He obligated Himself to become our Rescuer.

From the very beginning, the concepts of creation and redemption were linked together. When my mother

The Rescuer

had a child in her image, she pledged herself to rescue me when necessary. She was, and is, my rescuer. My mother would not have even entertained the thought of leaving me in the middle of the fields just because I

> *W*hen God created us in *His image,* He pledged Himself to a *rescue plan* because He was our *"closest of Kin."* He is our *Go'el*. He obligated Himself to become our Rescuer.

had became handicapped! No! She was my *mother*! And my rescuer. God is our Father and Redeemer (*Go'el*) and He wouldn't do that either: "You, O LORD, are our Father, our Redeemer [*Go'el*] from of old is Your name" (Isaiah 63:16).

Go'el is used in the Scriptures as a descriptive name for God, usually translated as Redeemer in our English Bibles. It highlights His mighty acts of redemption on behalf of His people (see Exodus 6:6; 15:13). Especially in the book of Isaiah, God constantly reminds us that He is our Kinsman-Redeemer, our *Go'el*. I am particularly touched when He reminds us to "fear not" because He has done His job as our *Go'el:*

> But now, thus says the LORD, your Creator, O Jacob,
> And He who formed you, O Israel,
> "Do not fear, for I have redeemed you;
> I have called you by name; you are Mine!" (Isaiah 43:1).

Surprised by *Love*

Jesus would be the One to become flesh, become our Brother, and redeem us without money (see Isaiah 52:3). He redeemed us with His blood; He came to die. That was the purpose—to pay the ransom because He is our *Go'el*. Jesus Himself stated that this was the purpose of His death, and in His explanation, we find a word usu-

> *D*o not fear, for I have redeemed you;
> I have called you by name; you are Mine!"

ally associated with the *Go'el* and the payment that was offered for the enslaved relative: "For even the Son of Man did not come to be served, but to serve, and to give His life a *ransom* for many" (Mark 10:45; see Revelation 21 and 22). Jesus redeemed us, He redeemed our land. (The new earth will be right here, we'll be back to where we started in Genesis 1! See Revelation 22.) Jesus fulfills all the roles of the *Go'el*. Praise God for our Kinsman-Redeemer!

If your children were kidnapped, wouldn't you pay the ransom, or do whatever was necessary to reclaim them? The whole Bible is a story of how God got His children back. You see, when humans chose to follow the kidnapper, they became sinful and mortal (see Romans 5:12–21). They were handicapped. They could not save themselves. They were dying, because "the wages of sin is death" (Romans 6:23). The deceitful serpent could never have imagined that God would love us this much! The deceiver thought that he had outsmarted God, that it was over! He never expected that love would win! Perhaps, humans themselves thought that they were beyond RE-DEMPTION! But "where sin increased, grace abounded all the more" (Romans 5:20). We were all surprised by LOVE! We beheld the unexpected rescue of God's children. Our *Go'el* stepped in.

Unexpected? Well, maybe, unless you are a parent. Then you get a glimpse as you think about it. "What would I do if my child, who is in my image, were in trouble, kidnapped, harmed, without hope, and had no way to save himself?"

> *I*f your children were kidnapped, wouldn't you pay the ransom, or do whatever was necessary to reclaim them? The whole Bible is a story of how God got His children back.

There comes a time when a parent has to do what a parent has to do! And God did! He stepped in, ran for His children, died for them, paid the ransom for them, and carried them to FREEDOM! We are free indeed!

My Redeemer lives!

I really don't understand why it is so hard for most of us to grasp this reality. Many of us have lived for a very long time with the fear that God doesn't like us, doesn't want us, or doesn't reach out to us. We come up with all kinds of rescue plans to earn His favor. Perhaps, if we were good enough, He might look upon us with approval, and maybe, just maybe, if we were really good, He might even come to love us. That is NOT the picture of God presented in the Bible! God is a Father, who, having lost

There comes a time when a parent has to do what a parent has to do! And God did!

His children to a kidnapper, refuses to go through eternity without them! He desperately wants to save them! Because He is the Creator who made them in His image, He designed a rescue plan. He became their Redeemer (*Go'el*) and paid the costly ransom. Sometimes I wonder how much it hurts God when we imply that what He did was not enough.

I know a couple who had been discussing their financial situation in order to make some decisions as money was tight. They were moving to another place and wanted to do some extra planning. Without them knowing, their

God is a Father, who, having lost His children to a kidnapper, refuses to go through eternity without them!

child had overheard their conversation. After a few hours, the parents noticed that the child seemed worried and anxious, so they asked him what was wrong. Their son went on to explain how he was worried that they would not be able to afford to feed him, to clothe him, or to provide shelter for him. He had made those conclusions from the overheard conversation of his parents. The parents felt so bad! They assured him that they would take care of him, that he had nothing to worry about! They assured him that he was their priority and that he was safe because they were taking full responsibility for him and all his needs!

Sometimes I imagine God's sad face when we are worried and anxious about our salvation. He doesn't have to ask. He knows that we are wondering if our salvation is sure, if we need to add something to what He has already done. I can almost picture tears in His eyes when we doubt the fact that He can really take care of us, that the ransom He paid is sufficient! Let me tell you once and for all: IT IS MORE THAN SUFFICIENT! He offered Himself as a sacrifice for the sins of all time (see Hebrews 10:12). Our salvation is secured! It is completed! Our *Go'el* has *done* His job!

Try to find a little cross and place a pushpin or a nail in the center. Write a paper note that reads, "PAID IN

> *I* can almost picture tears in His eyes when we doubt the fact that He can really take care of us, that the ransom He paid is sufficient!

FULL," sign it *"Go'el,"* and pin it to the cross. Place this visual aid somewhere where you can see it often. And on those days in which you don't feel worthy of your salvation, remember your *Go'el*. And during those times when you feel proud and think you can earn your own salvation,

> *I* know that my Redeemer lives!"

think of your *Go'el*. And when you are depressed and think you have gone too far into sin to come back to God, recall your *Go'el*.

Let's join Job in his assertion; let's do it aloud, emphasizing each word:

"I know that my Redeemer lives!" (Job 19:25).

You are not destitute and you are not enslaved. Even though you were kidnapped, your Rescuer stepped in. In the moment you accept your *Go'el* and what He has done for you, you are free! "If the Son makes you free, you will be free indeed!" (John 8:36).

Woo-hoo!

Chapter 4

The Ransom

When I was a little girl, my parents took me to a city in Argentina named Córdoba.* My father, then a pastor, was attending workers' meetings in a hotel for a few days. My mother anticipated having a good time in the company of other pastors' wives, and we, the children, excitedly looked forward to spending every minute of the day playing in the hotel's swimming pool. I was three and was told in no uncertain terms that I was to stay in the shallow part of the pool at all times—NO EXCEPTIONS! The happy day finally arrived and I found myself in water bliss. As usual, I was obedient to my parents' instructions. (Yeah, right, my mother would probably interject at this point to set the record straight.) All of a sudden something unexpected happened to me. I found myself in water at the edge of the forbidden zone, and the bottom of the pool was very slippery. VERY SLIPPERY! Green and slimy. I started sliding towards the deep end of the pool as if I was in an underwater playground, except that this was no fun. I found myself exactly in the very place where my mother told me not to go; and now I knew, in my young three-year-old heart, that I would die because I had no way out.

But there was something else that my heart knew—if my mother saw me, she would rescue me. Somehow, in

*Much of the material in this chapter is from my book, *John: God Became Flesh,* published by Pacific Press®.

my young brain, I understood that my mother's love for me would oblige her to jump in and save me. But the problem was that she couldn't see me! I gathered all my strength and tried to jump up, pushing my feet against the bottom of the pool, but I was already under the water and only my hand would briefly appear above the surface and then disappear again. I tried it again and again. AND MY MOTHER SAW ME! Yes, she noticed my little fingers above the water and that was all she needed!

*B*ut there was something else that
my heart knew—if my mother saw me,
she would rescue me.

SHE DOVE INTO THE POOL! It didn't matter what she was wearing and who was watching. All that mattered to her was that her little girl was drowning and she had to save her. And she did save me! It took a while, though, for me to come back to my normal self. My mother didn't need to consult a parenting textbook to learn what to do in such circumstances (just imagine the ridiculous thought of looking through the table of contents for the chapter "What to Do When Your Child Falls in the Pool"). Her mother's instinct and love made her do what a mother does best: SAVE HER LITTLE GIRL!

In this chapter, we will continue our study of the unexpected rescue of God's children. To fully understand the ransom that our *Go'el* paid for us, I want us to study together two encounters with Jesus from the Gospels. The first one is about God's little girl; the

> *G*od's little girl ended up just like me, exactly where she was told not to go—in the deep end of the pool. And she was sure she would die because there was no way out.

second (see the next chapter) is about God's little boy. Both of these chapters will give us an overview of the cost of our rescue.

God's little girl ended up just like me, exactly where she was told not to go—in the deep end of the pool. And she was sure she would die because there was no way out. That is, until Jesus, her *Go'el,* showed up and changed the direction of the story.

The court

During the first century A.D., the story found in John 8:2–11 circulated in the early church on its own, from mouth to mouth, not in written form. Though the story is absent in the earliest manuscripts of John, it is found in later ones. Sometimes it is found elsewhere; for example, at the end of Luke 21 and also at the end of the Gospel of John. Most of the stories about Jesus circulated on their own during the period of *oral traditions,* when the followers of Jesus preserved the accounts, parables, sayings, miracles, and dialogues of Jesus through the word of mouth. Eventually, these oral traditions made their way into the written form.

I like the placement of this story in this particular spot of the Gospel of John for several reasons. First, it is significant that chapter 8 of John begins with the accusers suggesting that the adulterous woman be stoned to death, and it ends with the Jews picking up stones to stone Jesus Himself (verse 59). Furthermore, in this chapter, the woman who was to be condemned is set free; while the Jews, who

> *T*hey REALLY want to make an example out of her, and so they take her to the very center of the temple court where everyone can see her.

didn't believe they needed to be set free, end up rejecting the only real Source of freedom: "If the Son makes you free, you will be free indeed" (verse 36), and thereby condemned themselves. I also find it fascinating that this story fits in perfectly with the immediate conglomeration of stories that seem to contrast Jesus with Moses, as if one had to decide to either be a disciple of Moses or a disciple of Jesus (see John 6:30–58; 7:19–24; 9:1–41). Eventually, in the next chapter (John 9:28, 29), the Pharisees proclaim themselves disciples of Moses and reject Jesus because of Sabbath keeping (something interesting to think about).

Our story takes place in the temple: "Early in the morning He came again into the temple, and all the people were coming to Him; and He sat down and began to teach them" (John 8:2). The scribes and Pharisees in the narrative appear eager to humiliate this woman caught in adultery. They could have kept her in custody elsewhere while speaking with Jesus. But they REALLY want to make an example out of her, and so they take her to the very center of the temple court where everyone can see her (see verse 3). Now the court of the temple becomes a court of law, as the accusers bring a legal question to Jesus. It was a routine procedure to take such cases to a rabbi for a decision. But Jesus was no ordinary Rabbi— He was her *Go'el*.

The charge

The charge against this woman is clear: *adultery*. The Jewish law required witnesses in order to make such charge; therefore, the narrative clearly states that this

When was the last time you went to church with a Bible in one hand and stones in the other?

woman was caught "in the very act" (verse 4). Adultery was one of the three gravest sins for a Jew; they would rather die than find themselves caught in idolatry, murder, or adultery. Next, the scribes and the Pharisees refer to the Law of Moses: "Now in the Law Moses commanded us to stone such women; what then do You say?" (verse 5).

Interesting, isn't it? When was the last time you went to church with a Bible in one hand and stones in the other? I know of churches where this seems to happen. Hopefully, your church is not one of them.

There are two main places in the Pentateuch that deal with such laws: Leviticus 20:10 and Deuteronomy 22:22–24. Leviticus 20:10 states, "If there is a man who commits adultery with another man's wife, one who commits adultery with his friend's wife, the adulterer and the adulteress shall surely be put to death." In this instance, if a man has sexual relations with the wife of a neighbor, both shall be put to death; the method is not identified. In Deuteronomy 22, the law states that "if there is a girl who is a virgin engaged to a man, and another man finds her in the city and lies with her, then you shall bring them both out to the gate of that city and you shall stone them to death" (verses 23, 24). The Law of Moses required stoning only when the girl was a virgin engaged to be married. There is no mention of

> God's little girl is in the bottom of the pool, and she is under the death penalty because of that.

such being the case, neither is there a man present to receive the death penalty too, and this is not taking place at the gate of the city (by the way, they are still in the court of the temple). There is no doubt that the scribes and the Pharisees are manipulating the law a bit. The narrative tells us that their motive is to test Jesus

The Ransom

"so that they might have grounds for accusing Him" (John 8:6). But the truth is, apart from all the excuses and manipulations of her accusers, SHE IS GUILTY! She is as guilty as it gets!

God's little girl is in the bottom of the pool, and she is under the death penalty because of that.

Have your children ever been in trouble or been sick and you just wished you could take their place? Well, picture your beloved child, your little girl, sitting in the middle of the court, with a death sentence on her head. As a matter of fact, all of us are there! We are all as guilty as this child of God! Let's place ourselves right beside her in the center of the court, condemned, without a way out, knowing that we deserve to die. "All have sinned and fall short

*O*nly those of us who understand the bad news can rejoice with the good news of our rescue!

of the glory of God" (Romans 3:23). It is so important for us to understand that the kidnapper deceived the whole human race and that we all became mortals, condemned to die. So, do you see yourself there in the center of the court? If you do, continue reading. NOW you are ready to experience what the adulterous woman (God's little girl, created in His image) experienced that day. Only those of us who understand the bad news can rejoice with the good news of our rescue!

Verdict: Guilty!

So, there is Jesus. The trap is cleverly set. The dilemma is this: the Jews had no power to carry out death sentences under Roman law (see John 18:31). So, if Jesus had said, "Go ahead! Stone her," then they would have brought a charge against Him with the Roman authorities. If Jesus had said, "No! Leave her alone," then they would have accused Him of teaching against the Law of Moses and would have discredited Jesus as a Rabbi. Pretty clever, wasn't it?

Jesus wrote something on the ground (see John 8:6). This is the only time recorded in all four Gospels that Jesus wrote anything. And I wish the narrative told us what He wrote! But it doesn't. A suggestion emerges from later manuscripts that add that He wrote "the sins of each one of them" (see verses 6 and 8). This claim could be substantiated by the fact that the Greek word for "to write" is *graphō,* but John 8:6 uses *katagraphō*—one of its meanings is to write down a record against someone, as *kata* can mean "against." However, it can also simply

*C*an you feel the intensity of the moment, right there in the center of the court? Are you afraid? Are you covering your head?

mean "wrote down" because He was writing on the ground. Whatever the case may be, the verdict Jesus pronounced is clear: "He who is without sin among you, let him be the first to throw a stone at her" (verse 7).

The Ransom

Can you feel the intensity of the moment, right there in the center of the court? Are you afraid? Are you covering your head? Really, how do you prepare to be stoned? By the way, there was a news piece some time ago about the stoning of an adulterous man somewhere in Africa. They buried him in the ground, leaving only his shoulders and head above ground—terrible even to think about not even being able to use your hands to cover your head!

Jesus simply specified those who were qualified to carry out the sentence: those who were without sin or sinful desires. These legal experts were conscience-stricken and began to leave one by one (see verse 9) while Jesus was still writing on the ground (see verse 8). No one was qualified! Not even one! No wait, that's wrong. ONE did qualify! And He was left alone with her: "He was left alone, and the woman, where she was, in the center of the court" (verse 9).

BY HIS OWN DEFINITION, JESUS WAS THE ONLY ONE WHO COULD THROW THE STONES! Get ready! The stones are coming! We are about to die! Your child is about to die! We all deserve it!

The ransom

"Jesus said to her, 'Woman, where are they? Did no one condemn you?' She said, 'No one, Lord.' And Jesus said, 'I do not condemn you, either. Go. From now on sin no more' " (verses 10, 11). WHAT? NOT CONDEMNED? What do you mean? HOW DARE Jesus do that? Does He not care about the law? Isn't the finger that wrote on the ground the same finger that wrote the law?

You see, the *Go'el,* the closest relative, could show up at court to make sure everything happened as it was supposed to. The only One qualified to throw the stone was also her *Go'el.* It was God's little girl sitting in that court, anticipating the shower of stones. What would YOU do if she was your little girl?

Well, that's exactly what Jesus did. In order to understand this completely, let's place a sign on this scene that says, "TO BE CONTINUED" because it is not over yet. Jesus, the ONLY ONE who was qualified to throw the

> *I*t was God's little girl sitting in that court,
> anticipating the shower of stones. What
> would YOU do if she was your little girl?
> Well, that's exactly what Jesus did.

stone, aborted this stoning. But a few days later, He picked up the stones and submitted Himself to be *stoned* by God (*crushed,* see Isaiah 53:10); and by doing so, He took the penalty upon Himself that belonged to her— that belongs to us all.

When Jesus was hanging on the cross, He said, "It is FINISHED!" (John 19:30). What was FINISHED? All condemnation for those who believe in Jesus was FINISHED because the sinless Son of God took humanity's death penalty upon Himself. So, let's place another sign, one that reads, "IT IS FINISHED" on this second scene, and you will have the complete picture of the ransom that was paid on behalf of God's children—on behalf of all of us. The whole sacrificial system of the Jewish Scriptures was pointing to this very moment. No wonder that in the first chapter of this Gospel (John 1:29) Jesus is introduced as "the Lamb of God who takes away the sin of the world!"

Jesus always speaks to us in the same order. First, "I

> *He* never says, "Sin no more, and then I won't condemn you."

do not condemn you"; then, "Go. . . . Sin no more." God wants us to live healthier lives for His glory and for our happiness, but He never reverses the order. He never says, "Sin no more, and then I won't condemn you." He already paid our death penalty on the cross. John is very specific about the purpose of God becoming flesh: "For God did not send the Son into the world to judge the world, but that the world might be saved through Him" (John 3:17).

Jesus jumped into the pool. And He saved us because He is our *Go'el.*

Wouldn't you have done the same for your little girl?

This guilty woman, sitting in the middle of the court, represents the whole human race. There are many days, sometimes weeks, months, and years, when we feel condemned, guilty as charged. Sometimes, other people condemn us; sometimes, we condemn ourselves. Guilt is heavy and it disables us by not allowing us to become who God designed us to be. I exhort you, in the name of Jesus Christ, to be free today. His sacrifice is sufficient!

> *W*ouldn't you have done the same
>
> for your little girl?

He paid the ransom!

Jesus announced this Himself. Let's take Him at His word! Place your name in the blank space: "The Son of Man did not come to be served, but to serve, and to give His life a ransom for _____" (Mark 10:45). Yep! He paid your ransom so that He could have you back with Him for eternity!

Like I said before, wouldn't you have done the same thing for your little girl?

$\mathcal{T}$he Assurance

One of the most inspiring stories that I have heard in the last few decades is the account of a father-son team, Dick and Rick Hoyt, who run marathons together. The amazing thing about them is the fact that the son, Rick, is a spastic quadriplegic with cerebral palsy. Most remarkably, every time they participate in a race, his father, Dick, pushes him in a wheelchair all the way to the finish line.

It all started in 1977, when Rick, then a young man, had asked his father to help him participate in a five-mile benefit run for a lacrosse player who was paralyzed in an accident. (Can you imagine Rick's compassionate heart?) His father agreed and pushed Rick in a wheelchair. When they had finished that first race, Rick wanted to say something to his dad, but he can't talk, so he had to wait until they got home. Once they arrived, he could communicate because, even though his extremities and lips do not obey him, he has a headpiece attached to his chair through which he can type into a computer to communicate. He wrote down, "Dad, when I'm running, it feels like I'm not handicapped." Dick got so excited about this new discovery that he started training systematically, so that his son could participate in many races and he could bring him to many finish lines. Dick loved his son very much and wanted him to know that and to experience life to the fullest! He wanted his son to know how important he was to him!

Since that first run, they have participated in more than a thousand races and are still running races today. If you want to learn more about this amazing family, visit their Web site at www.teamhoyt.com. You will be enchanted by photos of Rick's smile as they run. And it is heartwarming to see Dick's efforts as he works so hard to help his son, who can't run for himself. For me, the story came to a climax when I saw a documentary on the Hoyt team participating in the Ironman Triathlon in Hawaii. The father took his son through 112 miles of biking, 26.2 miles of running, and 2.4 miles of swimming so that Rick might experience the thrill of the race and know that he is worth every bit of Dick's effort! Rick will always be a winner, not because he is a strong and able athlete, but because his father, Dick, always takes him to

> *J*esus was hanging on a cross, and
> next to Him was God's little boy,
> hanging on another one.

the finish line! Seeing Dick transfer the fragile body of his son from the inflatable boat, which he had pulled, to the chair attached to his bicycle, in which Rick sits while his father pedals, has brought tears to my eyes literally dozens of times.

Rick is a very bright young man. In 1993, he graduated from Boston University with a degree in special education. Dick is a very devoted father, who, having served for thirty-seven years in the Air National Guard, retired in 1995 as a lieutenant colonel. Dick is looking forward to participating in the 2011 Boston Marathon with his son; he will be seventy years old by then!

The son is totally dependent on his father, there is absolutely no way for him to get to the finish line by himself. The story has become a powerful enacted parable for me, demonstrating the way my salvation was achieved. If an earthly father's love can be manifested in such an incredible way, how much more would our heavenly Father do to rescue His children and take them to the finish line? In this chapter, we will study one of the most amazing dialogues between God and His children: Jesus was hanging on a cross, and next to Him was God's little boy, hanging on another one. And Jesus is about to tell him what a Father's love is capable of.

The mockery

Please take a moment to read this fascinating dialogue; it is found in Luke 23:32–43. Done? OK. Let's start from the beginning: "Two others also, who were criminals, were being led away to be put to death with Him. When they came to the place called The Skull, there they crucified Him and the criminals, one on the right and the other on the left" (Luke 23:32, 33). Yes, Jesus was crucified along with two criminals, fulfilling the prophecy: "He poured out Himself to death, and was numbered with the transgressors" (Isaiah 53:12).

Surprised by *Love*

The place where they brought the three of them was called "The Skull," or in Latin "Calvaria," which is where we get the word *Calvary.* The names of the criminals are not specified in this narrative; all we know is that both are evildoers. The Greek word for "criminal," *kakourgos,*

> *They* didn't know they were crucifying their
> *Go'el,* their Kinsman-Redeemer, their closest
> of Kin, their only hope.

is composed of two words: *kakos* (evil, bad, wrong) and *ergon* (work, deed, action). In the most literal sense of the word, both of them are "evil workers." And Jesus is in the middle of the two.

The first utterance of Jesus from the cross is one of forgiveness: "Father, forgive them; for they do not know what they are doing" (Luke 23:34). They didn't know they were crucifying their *Go'el,* their Kinsman-Redeemer, their closest of Kin, their only hope. Perhaps you get a little glimpse of the depth of this heartfelt prayer when your teenager yells at you in a sudden burst of anger and tells you that he hates you! At that moment, he doesn't realize how excitedly you waited for his birth, how lovingly you arranged his nursery room, how tirelessly you fed him and changed his diapers, how patiently you taught him to walk, how selflessly you provided for his every need, and how you spared nothing, not even your own well-being, sitting by his side when he was sick and hurting. Don't you ever whisper in the middle of his angry outbursts, "Oh, Lord, forgive him; he doesn't know what he is saying, he doesn't understand"?

While Jesus intercedes, asking His Father to forgive them, "they cast lots, dividing up His garments among themselves" (Luke 23:34). Without realizing it, they were fulfilling the prophecy recorded in Psalm 22:18.

The people stare. But the rulers and the soldiers mock Jesus. Romans and Jews are united in their sneering, also fulfilling a prophecy. (See Psalm 22:7, 8. This is the psalm of the Righteous Sufferer; read it all in order to understand the force of the prophetic utterance regarding Jesus' crucifixion.) Jesus is dying the death of a traitor, and the legal charge "KING OF THE JEWS" is placed above Him (verse 38). The verb *to save* is brought up four times in this scene and is used as a mockery of Jesus' seeming inability to save Himself. As a matter of fact, a contrasting juxtaposition is constantly raised by those who mock Him. If He is the Christ, the Chosen One, the real King of the Jews, then He should have the ability to save Him-

> *J*esus is dying the death of a traitor, and the legal charge "KING OF THE JEWS" is placed above Him.

self. Well, this is the genius of Luke's story collecting and retelling: the reality is exactly the opposite! Jesus' identity as King and Savior is intertwined because His royal identity is sealed through His suffering to save others. This is the irony of the dialogue: Jesus is the King, the Messiah who accomplished the divine purpose of rescuing God's children. That was the PLAN! Surprise!

Surprised by Love: the unexpected rescue of God's children was happening right before their eyes, but no one could recognize it! Except one.

The unexpected request

In the midst of the mockery, a contrasting and unexpected voice is heard. Both "workers of evil" are speaking. The first criminal had been sarcastically insulting Jesus, joining the mockery. He was saying, "Are You not

> *S*urprised by Love: the unexpected rescue of God's children was happening right before their eyes, but no one could recognize it! Except one.

the Christ? Save Yourself and us!" (verse 39). But now the other evildoer responds with a rebuke, "Do you not even fear God, since you are under the same sentence of condemnation? And we indeed are suffering justly, for we are receiving what we deserve for our deeds; but this man has done nothing wrong" (verses 40, 41). His voice, in contrast to the mocking voices, presents two overwhelming truths: the criminals are suffering justly, and Jesus is suffering unjustly. They are guilty; Jesus is innocent. Their condemnation is righteous; but the Righteous One is under condemnation.

And then, without warning, the man with the dissenting voice turns to Jesus and utters the most outrageous and unexpected request you and I have ever heard! "Jesus, remember me when You come in Your kingdom!" (Luke 23:42).

What? What are you talking about? Don't you remember WHO you are? You are a *KAKOURGOS*! On what basis should Jesus remember YOU in His kingdom? The only way you will be remembered is as the notorious criminal who got what he deserved! Well, before we get too carried away, let's try to understand the request.

First of all, the criminal calls Christ by His name: *Jesus*. He did not call Him Rabbi or Messiah or Lord; he called Him *Jesus*, a name that, by its own definition, recalls that "Yahweh saves" (*Jesus* is the Greek version of the Hebrew name *Joshua*). The echo of the angelic announcement rings in our ears: "You shall call His name

> *And then*, without warning, the man with the dissenting voice turns to Jesus and utters the most outrageous and unexpected request you and I have ever heard!

Jesus, for He will save His people from their sins" (Matthew 1:21). The name by which the criminal addresses Jesus is in itself a remembrance of salvation!

The second part of the request is, "Remember me." This type of request was usually addressed to Yahweh in the Jewish Scriptures. When Yahweh remembered somebody, it didn't mean that the person was just coming back to His mind—it carried the blessing of His action on behalf of His people in keeping with His covenant. There are many examples of such requests to Yahweh (see Judges 16:28; 1 Samuel 1:11). So, this request is not about Jesus having memories of him, but about Jesus acting on his behalf.

In the Gospel of Luke, the poor, the outcast, the destitute, and the marginalized people have great insight regarding Jesus' identity. They seem to "get it" much more than the religious people because the marginalized know their need while those representing the religious system often don't. Luke is very deliberate about pointing this reality out in his narratives, encounters, and parables,

> *He* had come to understand that beyond the
>
> cross was the kingdom.

consistently presenting the ones without status and the marginalized as more insightful than anybody else. This is no exception. The important people such as the Romans and the Jewish rulers had continuously mocked Jesus, even requesting the release of Barabbas in His place (see Luke 23:13–25). Now, this insignificant criminal makes a request that reveals a deep understanding about Jesus' status and identity.

The third part of the request, "When You come in Your kingdom!" shows that this criminal had come to believe that the Crucifixion was not the end of Jesus.

Furthermore, he had come to understand that beyond the cross was the kingdom, and that in fact, Christ's suffering was consistent with His kingship, not contrary to it. Perhaps this man was the only witness of Jesus' death who understood that the charge against Jesus, which was inscribed on His cross, was a fulfillment of prophecy about His suffering. But why would Jesus even listen to him? Perhaps He shouldn't even respond! After all, *kakourgos* don't deserve any good promises, do they? Well, unless that person is your little boy, and you are his closest of kin.

The surprising response

Jesus answers with the eagerness of a parent responding to the desperate request of a child. But His response is so surprising that no one present in the scene could have anticipated it! It's hard to find an adequate contemporary equivalent to His response. But let's give it a try. Imagine that your child, who has just brought home a report of a failing grade and has managed to completely mess up his life and yours, makes a request that you purchase a car for him! Have you ever received such a ridiculous request? It would surprise everyone including yourself if you actually did go and get such a huge gift for your undeserving and misbehaving child! But what about if you said, "A car? No! Why would I want to get you just a car? I will rather give you a brand-new red Ferrari and a garage to go with it and a spacious mansion, plus a monthly ten-million-dollar allowance, forever, throughout eternity!" How about that kind of response?

Well that's exactly how Jesus responded, "Truly I say to you today you shall be with Me in Paradise" (Luke 23:43). The response starts with a "truly" ("amen" in the Greek), highlighting the veracity and the importance of the assurance about to be given. Jesus continued with *"I say to you,"* bringing into focus the subject and the object of the response. In other words, Jesus is saying to this man, "I am the Source of the assurance and you are the recipient."

What follows next is the most surprising response, which is only narrated in the Gospel of Luke, the core theological theme of which highlights the "salvation for all." We will distinguish four sections in Jesus' response.

*I*magine that your child, who has just brought home a report of a failing grade and has managed to completely mess up his life and yours, makes a request that you purchase a car for him! Have you ever received such a ridiculous request?

But before we go to these sections, let's review the order of the words in the original Greek, because that will help us determine the force of each word in the sentence. The original Greek reads with the following word order: "Truly to you I say today with Me you will be in Paradise."

Today. Jesus didn't want this man to wonder about his fate until Jesus came in His kingdom. No! This criminal could have the assurance of salvation today, at that very moment, without waiting one more second. No anxiety, no uncertainty. Just assurance—today! The word *today*

> *You will be.* Not, you might be, or let me think if you will be.

highlights the immediacy of the assurance of salvation through Jesus' ministry (see also Luke 4:21; 19:9).

You will be. The assurance is given in the second person singular and in the future tense, and it is a sure thing! *You will be.* Not, you might be, or let me think if you will be. That very day God's little boy could have the assurance that he was going to spend eternity with his *Go'el.* This was not the end for him, even though it surely looked like it. His presence with Jesus in His kingdom was not a possibility. It was a reality! Woohoo! I would give everything I have (which is not much) for every Christian to live with the assurance of salvation. What would it take for us to believe that we will be with Jesus?

Paradise. Jesus said, "You will be in Paradise"! Paradise! Remember? The nursery God made for His children! The place He created for their delight! The special Garden where the tree of life was! Remember? The very place God's children lost back in Genesis 3? Wow! This criminal is the first to be promised a bite from the fruit of the tree of life! He will be in Paradise! The Greek word used in Genesis 2–3 is *paradeisō.* (The Jewish Scriptures were translated into the Greek language; the translation was called the Septuagint or LXX. The New Testament writers, when referencing the Old Testament, used this

> *J*esus said, "You will be in Paradise"! Paradise! Remember? The nursery God made for His children! The place He created for their delight!

translation.) This is the place! Back with the Creator! All because of His love for us and the ransom paid by our *Go'el*.

At this very moment, Jesus, our *Go'el*, was paying the ransom. He had the authority to promise Paradise because He was paying for the criminal's sins, and for yours and mine. This is the only time in all four Gospels that Jesus utters the word *Paradise*! At this very moment, He

> *A*t this very moment, Jesus, our *Go'el*, was paying the ransom.

was opening up a way back home for His children, the way back to the tree of life, while taking upon Himself the death penalty they deserved. He had chosen to offer His perfect life (which none of us have) as a ransom for His children. And now He could promise Paradise! And His little boy, being crucified next to Him, was the first recipient of that promise! Surprise! Paradise! The way home has been re-opened! But at what cost!

With Me. Perhaps you noticed that I have skipped this phrase so far, contrary to the sequential order of the Greek manuscript. That is because in Greek, the weight

> *A*nd His little boy, being crucified next to Him, was the first recipient of that promise! Surprise! Paradise!

of the content is in the middle of the sentence. The core is in the center. I wanted to leave this important part to the last. And the center of Jesus' response is, "With Me." Jesus is saying to him, "All of the above is true, My little child, because you will be with Me. I am your ticket to Paradise, because at this very moment, I am carrying you to the finish line. You will be in Paradise because you are with Me. It is not because of your grades that you are getting the Ferrari, the mansion, and the million dollar allowance! No! It's because you are with Me. Do you understand? That is why it is in the middle of the sentence. I AM your assurance!"

"With Me" assurance

Some time ago, there was a program on TV where a preacher was describing his experience. He was part of a very important group accompanying a high-profile religious-political figure on a trip to the Middle East where some significant talks were about to take place. He described in detail who the important person was and how the rest of them, including him, were just part of the accompanying group.

When they had arrived in the foreign country, the preacher briefly lost sight of the person he had come with. But the security was so tight that the bodyguards surrounding the high-profile individual kept everyone else at a distance, and the man telling the story found himself outside of the security circle. This preacher got desperate and tried to explain to everyone that he was part of the group, but to no avail. He started to fear that he might have to return to the United States without accomplishing what he had come to do, because he could not get in. Then something happened that he will never forget.

The person he had come with, who by then was already several hundred yards from him, stopped. He

> *I* am your ticket to Paradise, because at this very moment, I am carrying you to the finish line. You will be in Paradise because you are with Me."

turned around, looked at him, and announced in a loud voice: "He is with me!" At once, the tight circle of security parted just like the Red Sea, and the preacher could simply walk in the middle! Just because this important person had said, "With me."

The Assurance

One day the criminal will be walking the streets of gold in Paradise. Wait! Instead, let's say one day I will be walking the streets of gold. I am sure that many will wonder what I am doing there and how I got into heaven. Well, I can't wait for Jesus to turn around, and in a thunderous voice, reply, "SHE IS WITH ME." Woo-hoo! Wow! I get goose bumps just thinking about it! Don't you?

The Hoyt team video documentary from the Ironman Triathlon contains a song entitled "My Redeemer Lives."

> *W*ell, I can't wait for Jesus to turn around, and in a thunderous voice, reply, "SHE IS WITH ME."

What a fitting song for the incredible images of the father taking his son through the race to the finish line! That day on the cross, Jesus, our Redeemer, carried us through to the finish line and made us winners! He said it, "IT IS FINISHED!" (John 19:30; emphasis added).

If, having tried everything else, you realize that you have nothing left that would qualify you to return home to Paradise, pray the criminal's prayer. You will receive the same response! Let's personalize the request, shall we? Fill in the blanks with your name:

"Jesus, remember me, _____,
when You come in Your kingdom!"

Surprised by *Love*

"Truly I say to you, _____
today, with Me you, _____, will
be in Paradise."

After all, wouldn't you have said the same to your
little boy?

Chapter 6

The Reunion

November 1, 2010, is the date set for the trial of Brian David Mitchell, who was ruled competent to stand trial on March 1 of the same year. He is the primary suspect in the June 5, 2002, kidnapping of Utah teenager Elizabeth Smart. I have watched many news and video clips about this kidnapping as this case fascinated me from the very beginning.

Elizabeth was abducted from her own bedroom in Salt Lake City at the age of fourteen. Ed Smart, her father, went on television that same morning, pleading and begging the kidnapper to return his girl. She was found nine months later on March 12, 2003, eighteen miles from her home. During the nine month ordeal, the whole town was dressed up in blue ribbons, waiting for her safe return. Everyone was praying and hoping until that significant day when someone recognized Brian Mitchell from a sketch of the suspected kidnapper. He was accompanied by two women, one of them was Elizabeth.

The kidnapped girl, now twenty-one, gave her testimony in a federal court on October 1, 2009. She explained how, immediately after the kidnapping, Mitchell performed a mock marriage ceremony before sexually assaulting her. Furthermore, she testified that during the nine months of her captivity, no twenty-four-hour period passed without Mitchell raping her.

Surprised by *Love*

I was grateful and relieved when she was found on March 12, 2003. The signs that were placed all over the town celebrating her homecoming touched me deeply. Businesses were not advertising their products on their

> *I* imagined many signs in heaven with the same inscription: "Elizabeth, Welcome Home."

commercial signs; you would only read, "Elizabeth, Welcome Home" instead. I felt something very special when I read those signs, perhaps because it is also my name. Many times my mind went ahead to the day I will be reunited with my Creator and Redeemer. I imagined many signs in heaven with the same inscription: "Elizabeth, Welcome Home."

At the time of her recovery, I was deeply touched by her father's emotions and the statements he made. Three of his statements I transcribed word for word. The first one relates to other kidnapped children who have not yet been found. He said, "All of the children out there deserve to come home to their parents the way Elizabeth has come back to us!" Then he started crying. The second is his response to a reporter who asked him to describe the first moments when he knew for sure that Elizabeth was alive. How can you describe such a scene? He said that he was in the police car, with Elizabeth in his arms, and he called his wife: "You are not going to believe this [he was sobbing as he related the dialogue]! Elizabeth is alive! And she is here in my arms!"

Then he said, "It is just the most wonderful, wonderful thing! As absolutely horrible as it was to have her taken, it is just absolutely wonderful to have her home again."

When the interview was over, I imagined God talking about us. I imagined His excitement about us being res-

> *Y*ou are not going to believe this [sobbing], Elizabeth is alive! And she is here in my arms!"

cued and reunited with Him forever. I had tears in my eyes when imagining Jesus, calling the Father, saying, "You are not going to believe this [sobbing], Elizabeth is alive! And she is here in my arms!"

This chapter relates the final reunion of God and His children. Yes! We are going home!

The Revelation of Jesus Christ

The last book of the Bible is the revelation of Christ as the ultimate Redeemer, victorious against the kidnapper. The book is introduced as the unveiling of Jesus: "The *Revelation of Jesus Christ,* which God gave Him to show to His bond-servants, the things which must soon take place; and He sent and communicated it by His angel to His bond-servant John" (Revelation 1:1; emphasis added). In this book, the kidnapper is exposed. "And the great dragon was thrown down, the serpent of old who is called the devil and Satan, who deceived the whole world" (Revelation 12:9). Remember the *serpent* that *deceived* the children of God back in Genesis 3? We know exactly who the kidnapper is and he is about to be no more.

This revelation (*apokalupsis,* which means "unveiling" or "disclosure") of Jesus is the last word of the Bible. It is written in apocalyptic style: a narrative genre that utilizes visualizations and symbols to convey the history of the plan of salvation from a "cosmic" perspective. It relates things from the past, things from the present, and things from the future (see Revelation 1:19). This literary genre was much more common during the time when the New Testament was written. In many ways, this book is a summary of the Bible. In its English versions, it contains a little more than four hundred verses; but it has more than five hundred allusions to the Old Testament. This means that

> This revelation (*apokalupsis,* which means "unveiling" or "disclosure") of Jesus is the last word of the Bible.

the author uses the main themes of the salvation history (for example, the plagues and the Exodus, the Exile and Babylon, and so forth) to demonstrate and announce the ultimate victory of our Redeemer over evil.

This book was written to encourage the faithful under difficult circumstances. John announces to his readers that the final showdown between our Redeemer and the kidnapper is imminent. But if they hang in there until the end, believing in the Lamb who was slain, they will spend eternity with God. This is a book of worship. Sixteen major worship scenes are portrayed in this unveiling narrative, where heaven and earth erupt in songs of exaltation, praising Him who has won victory through His blood. One of my favorite scenes of worship is the one narrated in Revelation 4 and 5. Could you pause for a

Jesus purchased our salvation with His blood, and this is how He rescued us from the deceitful kidnapper.

moment and read both chapters? Notice how many voices participate in this worship scene. The scene is rich with visualizations, including the Lion of the tribe of Judah who is the Lamb that was slain! And creatures and elders are singing a *new song*. I love the scenes, which are narrated in Revelation 5:6–10:

> And I saw between the throne (with the four living creatures) and the elders a Lamb standing, as if slain, having seven horns and seven eyes, which are the seven Spirits of God, sent out into all the earth. And He came and took the book out of the right hand of Him who sat on the throne. When He had taken the book, the four living creatures and the

twenty-four elders fell down before the Lamb, each one holding a harp and golden bowls full of incense, which are the prayers of the saints. And they sang a *new song,* saying,

"Worthy are You to take the book and to break its seals, for You were *slain,* and *purchased* for God with *Your blood* men from every tribe and tongue and people and nation.

"You have made them to be a kingdom and priests to our God; and they will reign upon the earth" (emphasis added).

Amen! Jesus purchased our salvation with His blood, and this is how He rescued us from the deceitful kidnapper. Oh, how much I want to be with Him! I can't wait until He comes for us!

Ending at the beginning

The whole Bible is an *inclusio.* This is an academic term for a "narrative sandwich," where something starts and ends in the same way. In the last three chapters of Revelation, we encounter the same themes that we saw in the first three chapters of the Bible, just in reversed order. This way, the Bible has symmetry. Remember the sequence of topics in Genesis 1–3: Creation (chapter 1), intimacy with God (chapter 2) and then the tempter, sin and evil, and death (chapter 3)? Well, the last three chapters of Revelation announce the reversal of those same things: Satan is bound and destroyed and sin and evil are no more (chapter 20); God once again dwells with His children, and there is no longer death or "mourning, or crying, or pain; the first things have passed away" (Revelation 21:4). The intimacy with God is restored (chapter 21). And finally, it gives a description of the re-created earth with all of the original attributes (chapter 22).

Most of the book of Revelation is about waiting for the exciting moment when our *Go'el* comes back to take us to be with Him. Can you imagine waiting for a long, *looong* time to see your children again? Ed Smart waited nine months to see his little girl again. God has been

*M*ost of the book of Revelation is about waiting for the exciting moment when our *Go'el* comes back to take us to be with Him.

waiting a lot longer. Can you imagine that moment? Ed couldn't contain his tears as he related the moment in which he had called his wife: "You are not going to believe this! Elizabeth is alive! And she is here in my arms!" Our *Go'el* came to this world the first time in order to pay our ransom. His birth and death are narrated in the Gospels. The Cross was the moment when we were set free. His perfect life, death, and resurrection assured eternal life for all those who accept the *Go'el*'s payment on their behalf. Now, the Redeemer is coming back as a triumphant Victor to take us home with Him. The description of the event is breathtaking:

Surprised by *Love*

And I saw heaven opened, and behold, a white horse, and He who sat on it is called Faithful and True, and in righteousness He judges and wages war. His eyes are a flame of fire, and on His head are many diadems; and He has a name written on Him which no one knows except Himself. He is clothed with a *robe dipped in blood,* and His name is called The Word of God (Revelation 19:11–13; emphasis added).

Wow! What a triumphant view of our Redeemer! He hardly resembles here the suffering Jesus, the One who was humiliated and mocked! But there is one reminder of the costly ransom that He paid in the midst of such a spectacular portrayal of His second coming: He is wearing a *robe dipped in blood*. His blood was the price He paid. And we will forever remember.

After a period of time specified as the "thousand years," the kidnapper, the serpent, "the devil who de-

> *He* is wearing a *robe dipped in blood*. His
> blood was the price He paid. And we will
> forever remember.

ceived them" (Revelation 20:10), is destroyed forever. Then the earth is re-created and becomes the new earth (see Revelation 21). It is very significant that our permanent home will be the same place where we were at the beginning, because this was one of the roles of the kinsman-redeemer. Remember how he had to redeem property that was given up by a poor relative? "If a fellow country-man of yours becomes so poor he has to sell part of his property, then his nearest kinsman [*Go'el*] is to come and buy back what his relative has sold" (Leviticus 25:25). Jesus, our Kinsman-Redeemer, not only rescued us through the ransom He paid, but He also got our land back (the earth) as well. Oh, this is just so exciting and wonderful! Beyond words! The Bible comes full circle through the blood of the Lamb!

Paradise restored!

As we open the book of Revelation, we immediately get into the language that was used at the beginning of the Jewish Scriptures; for example "to him who overcomes, I

> *I*t truly sounds and smells
> like home, doesn't it?

will grant to eat of the *tree of life* which is in the *Paradise* of God" (Revelation 2:7; emphasis added). *Tree of life* and *Paradise* are words we encountered in Genesis 2, when God prepared the ultimate "nursery" for His beloved children. The tree of life is also present in Genesis 3, with the sad reminder that humans would no longer have access to it because they were now mortals. But as we get to the place where the cosmic view of Jesus' ministry is unveiled, we start hearing this type of language again. It truly sounds and smells like home, doesn't it?

Surprised by *Love*

When we start reading Revelation 21, John announces that he "saw a new heaven and a new earth; . . . and there

> *The* presence of God with His people has been the theme throughout the history of humankind. They were created to be with Him. They are His children!

is no longer any sea" (verse 1). For the first century Mediterranean world, the sea was the place where evil resided. Evil is no more. And a loud voice from the throne is heard. This voice announces the fulfillment of the ongoing covenant theme that was spoken at different times and in different ways all through the Bible, always pointing to God dwelling with His people:

> And I heard a loud voice from the throne, saying, "Behold, the tabernacle of God is among men, and He will dwell among them, and they shall be His people, and God Himself will be among them, and He will wipe away every tear from their eyes; and there will no longer be any death; there will no longer be any mourning, or crying, or pain; the first things have passed away" (Revelation 21:3, 4).

The presence of God with His people has been the theme throughout the history of humankind. They were created to be with Him. They are His children! We are reminded of this throughout the Old Testament. "I will make My dwelling among you. . . . I will also walk among you and be your God, and you shall be My people" (Leviticus 26:11, 12).

Moreover, God designed a way in which His people would experience His presence: the tabernacle in the wilderness and, eventually, the temple. God manifested the glory of His presence in these sacred structures. When Jesus became flesh, He *tabernacled* (it is the same word as *tabernacle* only in a verb form, usually translated as "dwelt") among us, and once again "we saw His glory,

God is finally back with His children, whom He lost in Paradise. Now they are back again.

At home in Paradise.

glory as of the only begotten from the Father, full of grace and truth" (John 1:14). Jesus was the ultimate representation of God's glory (see Hebrews 1:1–3). In the new earth, the tabernacle of God is among men because He is dwelling with them forever more. There is no more temple because God Himself is among them: "I saw no temple in it, for the Lord God the Almighty and the Lamb are its temple" (Revelation 21:22). God is finally back with His children, whom He lost in Paradise. Now they are back again. At home in Paradise.

The covenant of God was given to Adam, Noah, Abraham, Moses, and David in the Jewish Scriptures. These men of old received signs of the covenant and had glimpses of its developmental nature. When we get to the new earth, the covenant will be fulfilled and the ultimate reality for us will be that we will have received the *divine sonship*. We are, in fact, children of God! God will be with us and we will be with God! Reunited! Forever! The accomplishment of this final reality will be announced by God Himself:

> And He who sits on the throne said, "Behold, *I am making all things new*." And He said, "Write, for these words are faithful and true." Then He said to me, "*It is done. I am the Alpha and the Omega, the beginning and the end.* I will give to the one who thirsts from the spring of the water of life without cost. He who overcomes will inherit these things, *and I will be his God and he will be My son*" (Revelation 21:5–7; emphasis added).

Wow! It is a done deal! And our ultimate reality is the *divine sonship*! It is impossible to describe this reunion adequately. We can just imagine the voice declaring all of the benefits that will be ours when God dwells with His children forever. Think about it. Just the abolishment of the effects of sin alone should make your heart soar—death, crying, and pain—they are all history!

Back to the tree of life

The last book of the Bible ends with a scene of the redeemed humanity, returned to the tree of life. We have come full circle.

The Reunion

Then he showed me a river of the water of life, clear as crystal, coming from the throne of God and of the Lamb, in the middle of its street. On either side of the river was the tree of life, bearing twelve kinds of fruit, yielding its fruit every month; and the leaves of the tree were for the healing of the nations (Revelation 22:1, 2).

The same tree that God planted in Paradise in the beginning is back. Remember how Jesus promised Paradise to the criminal on the cross in the previous chapter?

Think about it. Just the abolishment of the effects of sin alone should make your heart soar—death, crying, and pain—they are all history!

Here we are, standing by the tree of life. Its fruit is described in vivid and luscious words.

Then John utters the seventh and last beatitude in this book: "*Blessed* are *those who wash their robes,* so that they may have *the right to the tree of life,* and may enter by the gates into the city" (Revelation 22:14; emphasis added). The expression of "washing their robes" has already been explained previously in Revelation: "They have *washed their robes* and made them white *in the blood of the Lamb*" (Revelation 7:14; emphasis added). Those who are now the blessed ones have the right to the tree of life, a symbol of immortality, *because* they have washed their robes in the blood of the Lamb; they accepted the ransom paid by their *Go'el*. This is the *only* reason why they have the right

> *Y*es, I am coming quickly." Do you hear the eagerness of a Parent coming back for His children?

to go back to the tree of life, which humans lost when they followed the kidnapper.

The last "red letters" in the Bible (direct words of Jesus) are recorded in Revelation 22:20, when the risen Christ speaks for the last time: "Yes, I am coming quickly." Do you hear the eagerness of a Parent coming back for His children? John's answer is also representative of the longing response all of us have to see our Redeemer and be with God forever: "Amen, Come, Lord Jesus" (verse 20). Amen! Come, Lord Jesus! Come soon!

I started this chapter describing the signs in Salt Lake City: "Elizabeth, Welcome Home!" Well, I can already imagine signs everywhere as we are getting closer to heaven: "Dear Children, Welcome Home!" I am crying

> *D*ear Children, Welcome Home!"

as I write these visualizations because I know He is coming for us! I can almost hear Jesus' voice, "They are alive! And they are here in My arms!"

The Reunion

This is not just a fairy tale. It is the real history of humankind from the beginning to eternity. It is the full circle from Creation to Redemption, only possible because a costly ransom was paid by our *Go'el*. Aren't you surprised by *this much* love? This is the story of the truly unexpected and *successful* rescue of God's kidnapped children.

And God and His children lived happily ever after! The End!

*W*oo-Hoo!

If you have been blessed by this booklet and would like to help us keep spreading the good news of Jesus Christ through preaching, teaching, and writing, please send your donations to

Voice of Prophecy
Attn: Jesus101 Biblical Institute
P. O. Box 941659
Simi Valley, CA 93094

www.vop.com